We the People

How the Constitution Applies to Today's Issues

Crawford Harris

eb essential books

We the People Copyright © 2019

by Crawford Harris All rights reserved

Except for those portions which are constituent parts of the Constitution itself, no part of this book may be reproduced in any manner whatsoever without the written permission of the author, except for brief quotations as a part of critical articles or reviews.

We the People by Crawford Harris

April 2019

Printed in USA

Set in Palatino Linotype

eb essential books

Contents

Dedication v

Acknowledgements vii

Preface ix

Introduction 1

The Constitution 5

The Bill of Rights 28

Amendments 11 thru 27 32

From the Top 43

Fear of Corporations 49

Welfare 53

Parts of the Government 55

Legislation 57

Democracy? 59

Emoluments 63

Pardon Me 67

Religion 69

The 2nd Amendment 73

States' Rights? 77

Shutting Down 79

From the Publisher 83

The Author 85

Dedication

To those who are fighting to get us closer to a true democracy and those struggling to cross the divides to find ways of helping us live together in harmony with our fellow human beings. *E pluribus unum.*

Acknowledgements

James Madison, Alexander Hamilton and a few others deserve some credit for their contributions.

Preface

Having been a foreign correspondent, I am a news addict. Needless to say, I don't see the changes in that profession over the past nearly sixty years as all positive. Still, I am addicted to the news. Next to my monitors, I usually have the television turned to a news channel

I was close to completion of this book when the president was holding a press scrum on his way to a helicopter. The apparently willful ignorance of our system of government was appalling. My feeling about the importance of understanding our system, our Constitution was reinforced.

He feigned ignorance of the position of prosecutors. He again claimed to have won the greatest election victory in the history of the country. He bragged that 63 million voters elected him. And here I was laboring under the misconception that it was the Electoral College that was the culprit.

He claimed that Special Counsel Mueller came out of nowhere and was writing a report. Why was he writing a report when nobody voted for him? He said that his voters couldn't understand that. And here I always thought that he was supposed to be the president of all the people. Perhaps he needs a copy of this.

The Constitution is not perfect but it has served us well in many ways – many, not all. It took too much time and bloodshed to rid ourselves of slavery. It took too much time to give women their due. It is taking too much time to cure other defects but it is our most valuable possession, as citizens. We owe it to ourselves to understand this document. As citizens, it is our duty.

Introduction

Everyone knows about the Constitution. Most don't really know the Constitution. They just know about it. That is an important distinction.

There are more than enough people running around today smugly characterizing themselves as 'strict constructionists' or 'originalists.' These are the people to be ignored at all costs.

Why?

Because the Founders knew that times would change. They realized that society would change. In fact, many wanted it to change. Some hoped that slavery would go away. Others desired other changes.

Most were less than fully satisfied with the final document. All realized that it was not exactly what they wanted. It was the result of compromise, many compromises. They hoped for the best; at least what they considered the best.

The expectation of change was the reason they included a couple of methods for changing it. In other words, the authors of the Constitution were no 'strict constructionists.' We can call them originals, but certainly not 'originalists.'

That should be sufficient reason to ignore or laugh at those styling themselves as such. They are ignorant of history. They are ignorant of the Constitution. And, sitting on the Supreme Court does not justify the pomposity of such intellectually limited people. Think Antonin Scalia or Clarence Thomas.

I intend to do something relatively rare, or perhaps even absent among those sitting in seats of power in our government. I will apply history, logic and literacy in my analysis. I will not address every article and section. My intent is to present the Constitution in its entirety but demonstrate how certain parts of it should be applied to some of our present-day issues.

I take my marching orders from the initial three words of the document that is supposed to define this nation. I suggest that any who disagree with

Introduction

me (surely there are a few) follow suit, at least while engaged in reading this. Upon completion, they are welcome to return to their former state and once again bask in their ignorance.

The spelling and punctuation follow, more or less, the way it was given to us.

First the Constitution, then the commentary.

The Constitution

We the People of the United States, in Order to form a more perfect Union, establish Justice, insure domestic Tranquility, provide for the common defence, promote the general Welfare, and secure the Blessings of Liberty to ourselves and our Posterity, do ordain and establish this Constitution for the United States of America.

Article I (Article 1 - Legislative)

Section 1

All legislative Powers herein granted shall be vested in a Congress of the United States, which shall consist of a Senate and House of Representatives.

Section 2

1. The House of Representatives shall be composed of Members chosen every second Year by the People of the several States, and the Electors in each State shall have the Qualifications requisite for Electors of the most numerous Branch of the State Legislature.

2. No Person shall be a Representative who shall not have attained to the Age of twenty five Years, and been seven Years a Citizen of the United States, and who shall not, when elected, be an Inhabitant of that State in which he shall be chosen.
3. Representatives and direct Taxes shall be apportioned among the several States which may be included within this Union, according to their respective Numbers, which shall be determined by adding to the whole Number of free Persons, including those bound to Service for a Term of Years, and excluding Indians not taxed, three fifths of all other Persons. The actual Enumeration shall be made within three Years after the first Meeting of the Congress of the United States, and within every subsequent Term of ten Years, in such Manner as they shall by Law direct. The Number of Representatives shall not exceed one for every thirty Thousand, but each State shall have at Least one Representative; and until such enumeration shall be made, the State of New Hampshire shall be entitled to chuse three, Massachusetts eight, Rhode-Island and Providence Plantations one, Connecticut five, New-York six, New Jersey four, Pennsylvania eight, Delaware one, Maryland six, Virginia ten, North Carolina five, South Carolina five, and Georgia three.
4. When vacancies happen in the Representation from any State, the Executive Authority thereof shall issue Writs of Election to fill such Vacancies.
5. The House of Representatives shall chuse their Speaker and other Officers; and shall have the sole Power of Impeachment.

The Constitution

Section 3

1. The Senate of the United States shall be composed of two Senators from each State, chosen by the Legislature thereof, for six Years; and each Senator shall have one Vote.
2. Immediately after they shall be assembled in Consequence of the first Election, they shall be divided as equally as may be into three Classes. The Seats of the Senators of the first Class shall be vacated at the Expiration of the second Year, of the second Class at the Expiration of the fourth Year, and of the third Class at the Expiration of the sixth Year, so that one third may be chosen every second Year; and if Vacancies happen by Resignation, or otherwise, during the Recess of the Legislature of any State, the Executive thereof may make temporary Appointments until the next Meeting of the Legislature, which shall then fill such Vacancies.
3. No Person shall be a Senator who shall not have attained to the Age of thirty Years, and been nine Years a Citizen of the United States, and who shall not, when elected, be an Inhabitant of that State for which he shall be chosen.
4. The Vice President of the United States shall be President of the Senate, but shall have no Vote, unless they be equally divided.
5. The Senate shall chuse their other Officers, and also a President pro tempore, in the Absence of the Vice President, or when he shall exercise the Office of President of the United States.
6. The Senate shall have the sole Power to try all Impeachments. When sitting for that Purpose, they shall

be on Oath or Affirmation. When the President of the United States is tried, the Chief Justice shall preside: And no Person shall be convicted without the Concurrence of two thirds of the Members present.

7. Judgment in Cases of impeachment shall not extend further than to removal from Office, and disqualification to hold and enjoy any Office of honor, Trust or Profit under the United States: but the Party convicted shall nevertheless be liable and subject to Indictment, Trial, Judgment and Punishment, according to Law.

Section 4

1. The Times, Places and Manner of holding Elections for Senators and Representatives, shall be prescribed in each State by the Legislature thereof; but the Congress may at any time by Law make or alter such Regulations, except as to the Places of chusing Senators.
2. The Congress shall assemble at least once in every Year, and such Meeting shall be on the first Monday in December, unless they shall by Law appoint a different Day.

Section 5

1. Each House shall be the Judge of the Elections, Returns and Qualifications of its own Members, and a Majority of each shall constitute a Quorum to do Business; but a smaller Number may adjourn from day to day, and may be authorized to compel the Attendance of absent Members, in such Manner, and under such Penalties as each House may provide.

2. Each House may determine the Rules of its Proceedings, punish its Members for disorderly Behaviour, and, with the Concurrence of two thirds, expel a Member.
3. Each House shall keep a Journal of its Proceedings, and from time to time publish the same, excepting such Parts as may in their Judgment require Secrecy; and the Yeas and Nays of the Members of either House on any question shall, at the Desire of one fifth of those Present, be entered on the Journal.
4. Neither House, during the Session of Congress, shall, without the Consent of the other, adjourn for more than three days, nor to any other Place than that in which the two Houses shall be sitting.

Section 6

1. The Senators and Representatives shall receive a Compensation for their Services, to be ascertained by Law, and paid out of the Treasury of the United States. They shall in all Cases, except Treason, Felony and Breach of the Peace, be privileged from Arrest during their Attendance at the Session of their respective Houses, and in going to and returning from the same; and for any Speech or Debate in either House, they shall not be questioned in any other Place.
2. No Senator or Representative shall, during the Time for which he was elected, be appointed to any civil Office under the Authority of the United States, which shall have been created, or the Emoluments whereof shall have been encreased during such time; and no Person holding any Office under the United States, shall be a Member of either House during his Continuance in Office.

Section 7

1. All Bills for raising Revenue shall originate in the House of Representatives; but the Senate may propose or concur with Amendments as on other Bills.
2. Every Bill which shall have passed the House of Representatives and the Senate, shall, before it become a Law, be presented to the President of the United States; If he approve he shall sign it, but if not he shall return it, with his Objections to that House in which it shall have originated, who shall enter the Objections at large on their Journal, and proceed to reconsider it. If after such Reconsideration two thirds of that House shall agree to pass the Bill, it shall be sent, together with the Objections, to the other House, by which it shall likewise be reconsidered, and if approved by two thirds of that House, it shall become a Law. But in all such Cases the Votes of both Houses shall be determined by yeas and Nays, and the Names of the Persons voting for and against the Bill shall be entered on the Journal of each House respectively. If any Bill shall not be returned by the President within ten Days (Sundays excepted) after it shall have been presented to him, the Same shall be a Law, in like Manner as if he had signed it, unless the Congress by their Adjournment prevent its Return, in which Case it shall not be a Law.
3. Every Order, Resolution, or Vote to which the Concurrence of the Senate and House of Representatives may be necessary (except on a question of Adjournment) shall be presented to the President of the United States; and before the Same shall take Effect, shall be approved by him, or being disapproved by him, shall be repassed by

two thirds of the Senate and House of Representatives, according to the Rules and Limitations prescribed in the Case of a Bill.

Section 8

1. The Congress shall have Power To lay and collect Taxes, Duties, Imposts and Excises, to pay the Debts and provide for the common Defence and general Welfare of the United States; but all Duties, Imposts and Excises shall be uniform throughout the United States;
2. To borrow Money on the credit of the United States;
3. To regulate Commerce with foreign Nations, and among the several States, and with the Indian Tribes;
4. To establish an uniform Rule of Naturalization, and uniform Laws on the subject of Bankruptcies throughout the United States;
5. To coin Money, regulate the Value thereof, and of foreign Coin, and fix the Standard of Weights and Measures;
6. To provide for the Punishment of counterfeiting the Securities and current Coin of the United States;
7. To establish Post Offices and post Roads;
8. To promote the Progress of Science and useful Arts, by securing for limited Times to Authors and Inventors the exclusive Right to their respective Writings and Discoveries;
9. To constitute Tribunals inferior to the supreme Court;
10. To define and punish Piracies and Felonies committed on the high Seas, and Offences against the Law of Nations;
11. To declare War, grant Letters of Marque and Reprisal, and make Rules concerning Captures on Land and Water;

12. To raise and support Armies, but no Appropriation of Money to that Use shall be for a longer Term than two Years;
13. To provide and maintain a Navy;
14. To make Rules for the Government and Regulation of the land and naval Forces;
15. To provide for calling forth the Militia to execute the Laws of the Union, suppress Insurrections and repel Invasions;
16. To provide for organizing, arming, and disciplining, the Militia, and for governing such Part of them as may be employed in the Service of the United States, reserving to the States respectively, the Appointment of the Officers, and the Authority of training the Militia according to the discipline prescribed by Congress;
17. To exercise exclusive Legislation in all Cases whatsoever, over such District (not exceeding ten Miles square) as may, by Cession of particular States, and the Acceptance of Congress, become the Seat of the Government of the United States, and to exercise like Authority over all Places purchased by the Consent of the Legislature of the State in which the Same shall be, for the Erection of Forts, Magazines, Arsenals, dock-Yards, and other needful Buildings; — And
18. To make all Laws which shall be necessary and proper for carrying into Execution the foregoing Powers, and all other Powers vested by this Constitution in the Government of the United States, or in any Department or Officer thereof.

Section 9

1. The Migration or Importation of such Persons as any of the States now existing shall think proper to admit, shall not be prohibited by the Congress prior to the Year one thousand eight hundred and eight, but a Tax or duty may be imposed on such Importation, not exceeding ten dollars for each Person.
2. The Privilege of the Writ of Habeas Corpus shall not be suspended, unless when in Cases of Rebellion or Invasion the public Safety may require it.
3. No Bill of Attainder or ex post facto Law shall be passed.
4. No Capitation, or other direct, Tax shall be laid, unless in Proportion to the Census or Enumeration herein before directed to be taken.7
5. No Tax or Duty shall be laid on Articles exported from any State.
6. No Preference shall be given by any Regulation of Commerce or Revenue to the Ports of one State over those of another: nor shall Vessels bound to, or from, one State, be obliged to enter, clear, or pay Duties in another.
7. No Money shall be drawn from the Treasury, but in Consequence of Appropriations made by Law; and a regular Statement and Account of the Receipts and Expenditures of all public Money shall be published from time to time.
8. No Title of Nobility shall be granted by the United States: And no Person holding any Office of Profit or Trust under them, shall, without the Consent of the Congress, accept of any present, Emolument, Office, or Title, of any kind whatever, from any King, Prince, or foreign State.

Section 10

1. No State shall enter into any Treaty, Alliance, or Confederation; grant Letters of Marque and Reprisal; coin Money; emit Bills of Credit; make any Thing but gold and silver Coin a Tender in Payment of Debts; pass any Bill of Attainder, ex post facto Law, or Law impairing the Obligation of Contracts, or grant any Title of Nobility.
2. No State shall, without the Consent of the Congress, lay any Imposts or Duties on Imports or Exports, except what may be absolutely necessary for executing it's inspection Laws: and the net Produce of all Duties and Imposts, laid by any State on Imports or Exports, shall be for the Use of the Treasury of the United States; and all such Laws shall be subject to the Revision and Controul of the Congress.
3. No State shall, without the Consent of Congress, lay any Duty of Tonnage, keep Troops, or Ships of War in time of Peace, enter into any Agreement or Compact with another State, or with a foreign Power, or engage in War, unless actually invaded, or in such imminent Danger as will not admit of delay.

Article II (Article 2 - Executive)

Section 1

1. The executive Power shall be vested in a President of the United States of America. He shall hold his Office during the Term of four Years, and, together with the Vice President, chosen for the same Term, be elected, as follows

2. Each State shall appoint, in such Manner as the Legislature thereof may direct, a Number of Electors, equal to the whole Number of Senators and Representatives to which the State may be entitled in the Congress: but no Senator or Representative, or Person holding an Office of Trust or Profit under the United States, shall be appointed an Elector.
3. The Electors shall meet in their respective States, and vote by Ballot for two Persons, of whom one at least shall not be an Inhabitant of the same State with themselves. And they shall make a List of all the Persons voted for, and of the Number of Votes for each; which List they shall sign and certify, and transmit sealed to the Seat of the Government of the United States, directed to the President of the Senate. The President of the Senate shall, in the Presence of the Senate and House of Representatives, open all the Certificates, and the Votes shall then be counted. The Person having the greatest Number of Votes shall be the President, if such Number be a Majority of the whole Number of Electors appointed; and if there be more than one who have such Majority, and have an equal Number of Votes, then the House of Representatives shall immediately chuse by Ballot one of them for President; and if no Person have a Majority, then from the five highest on the List the said House shall in like Manner chuse the President. But in chusing the President, the Votes shall be taken by States, the Representation from each State having one Vote; A quorum for this Purpose shall consist of a Member or Members from two thirds of the States, and a Majority of all the States shall be necessary to a Choice. In every Case, after the Choice of

the President, the Person having the greatest Number of Votes of the Electors shall be the Vice President. But if there should remain two or more who have equal Votes, the Senate shall chuse from them by Ballot the Vice President.

4. The Congress may determine the Time of chusing the Electors, and the Day on which they shall give their Votes; which Day shall be the same throughout the United States.

5. No Person except a natural born Citizen, or a Citizen of the United States, at the time of the Adoption of this Constitution, shall be eligible to the Office of President; neither shall any Person be eligible to that Office who shall not have attained to the Age of thirty five Years, and been fourteen Years a Resident within the United States.

6. In Case of the Removal of the President from Office, or of his Death, Resignation, or Inability to discharge the Powers and Duties of the said Office, the Same shall devolve on the Vice President, and the Congress may by Law provide for the Case of Removal, Death, Resignation or Inability, both of the President and Vice President, declaring what Officer shall then act as President, and such Officer shall act accordingly, until the Disability be removed, or a President shall be elected.

7. The President shall, at stated Times, receive for his Services, a Compensation, which shall neither be encreased nor diminished during the Period for which he shall have been elected, and he shall not receive within that Period any other Emolument from the United States, or any of them.

8. Before he enters on the Execution of his Office, he shall take the following Oath or Affirmation: — "I do solemnly

swear (or affirm) that I will faithfully execute the Office of President of the United States, and will to the best of my Ability, preserve, protect and defend the Constitution of the United States."

Section 2

1. The President shall be Commander in Chief of the Army and Navy of the United States, and of the Militia of the several States, when called into the actual Service of the United States; he may require the Opinion, in writing, of the principal Officer in each of the executive Departments, upon any Subject relating to the Duties of their respective Offices, and he shall have Power to grant Reprieves and Pardons for Offences against the United States, except in Cases of Impeachment.
2. He shall have Power, by and with the Advice and Consent of the Senate, to make Treaties, provided two thirds of the Senators present concur; and he shall nominate, and by and with the Advice and Consent of the Senate, shall appoint Ambassadors, other public Ministers and Consuls, Judges of the supreme Court, and all other Officers of the United States, whose Appointments are not herein otherwise provided for, and which shall be established by Law: but the Congress may by Law vest the Appointment of such inferior Officers, as they think proper, in the President alone, in the Courts of Law, or in the Heads of Departments.
3. The President shall have Power to fill up all Vacancies that may happen during the Recess of the Senate, by granting Commissions which shall expire at the End of their next Session.

Section 3

He shall from time to time give to the Congress Information of the State of the Union, and recommend to their Consideration such Measures as he shall judge necessary and expedient; he may, on extraordinary Occasions, convene both Houses, or either of them, and in Case of Disagreement between them, with Respect to the Time of Adjournment, he may adjourn them to such Time as he shall think proper; he shall receive Ambassadors and other public Ministers; he shall take Care that the Laws be faithfully executed, and shall Commission all the Officers of the United States.

Section 4

The President, Vice President and all civil Officers of the United States, shall be removed from Office on Impeachment for, and Conviction of, Treason, Bribery, or other high Crimes and Misdemeanors.

Article III (Article 3 - Judicial)

Section 1

The judicial Power of the United States, shall be vested in one supreme Court, and in such inferior Courts as the Congress may from time to time ordain and establish. The Judges, both of the supreme and inferior Courts, shall hold their Offices during good Behaviour, and shall, at stated Times, receive for their Services, a Compensation, which shall not be diminished during their Continuance in Office.

Section 2

1. The judicial Power shall extend to all Cases, in Law and Equity, arising under this Constitution, the Laws of the United States, and Treaties made, or which shall be made, under their Authority; — to all Cases affecting Ambassadors, other public Ministers and Consuls; — to all Cases of admiralty and maritime Jurisdiction; — to Controversies to which the United States shall be a Party; — to Controversies between two or more States; — between a State and Citizens of another State; —between Citizens of different States, — between Citizens of the same State claiming Lands under Grants of different States, and between a State, or the Citizens thereof, and foreign States, Citizens or Subjects.
2. In all Cases affecting Ambassadors, other public Ministers and Consuls, and those in which a State shall be Party, the supreme Court shall have original Jurisdiction. In all the other Cases before mentioned, the supreme Court shall have appellate Jurisdiction, both as to Law and Fact, with such Exceptions, and under such Regulations as the Congress shall make.
3. The Trial of all Crimes, except in Cases of Impeachment, shall be by Jury; and such Trial shall be held in the State where the said Crimes shall have been committed; but when not committed within any State, the Trial shall be at such Place or Places as the Congress may by Law have directed.

Section 3

1. Treason against the United States, shall consist only in levying War against them, or in adhering to their Enemies, giving them Aid and Comfort. No Person shall be convicted of Treason unless on the Testimony of two Witnesses to the same overt Act, or on Confession in open Court.
2. The Congress shall have Power to declare the Punishment of Treason, but no Attainder of Treason shall work Corruption of Blood, or Forfeiture except during the Life of the Person attainted.

Article IV (Article 4 - States' Relations)

Section 1

Full Faith and Credit shall be given in each State to the public Acts, Records, and judicial Proceedings of every other State. And the Congress may by general Laws prescribe the Manner in which such Acts, Records and Proceedings shall be proved, and the Effect thereof.

Section 2

1. The Citizens of each State shall be entitled to all Privileges and Immunities of Citizens in the several States.
2. A Person charged in any State with Treason, Felony, or other Crime, who shall flee from Justice, and be found in another State, shall on Demand of the executive Authority of the State from which he fled, be delivered up, to be removed to the State having Jurisdiction of the Crime.
3. No Person held to Service or Labour in one State, under the Laws thereof, escaping into another, shall, in

Consequence of any Law or Regulation therein, be discharged from such Service or Labour, but shall be delivered up on Claim of the Party to whom such Service or Labour may be due.

Section 3

1. New States may be admitted by the Congress into this Union; but no new State shall be formed or erected within the Jurisdiction of any other State; nor any State be formed by the Junction of two or more States, or Parts of States, without the Consent of the Legislatures of the States concerned as well as of the Congress.
2. The Congress shall have Power to dispose of and make all needful Rules and Regulations respecting the Territory or other Property belonging to the United States; and nothing in this Constitution shall be so construed as to Prejudice any Claims of the United States, or of any particular State.

Section 4

The United States shall guarantee to every State in this Union a Republican Form of Government, and shall protect each of them against Invasion; and on Application of the Legislature, or of the Executive (when the Legislature cannot be convened) against domestic Violence.

Article V (Article 5 - Mode of Amendment)

The Congress, whenever two thirds of both Houses shall deem it necessary, shall propose Amendments to this Constitution, or, on the Application of the Legislatures of two thirds of the several States, shall call a Convention for proposing Amendments, which, in either Case, shall be valid to all Intents and Purposes, as Part of this Constitution, when ratified by the Legislatures of three fourths of the several States, or by Conventions in three fourths thereof, as the one or the other Mode of Ratification may be proposed by the Congress; Provided that no Amendment which may be made prior to the Year One thousand eight hundred and eight shall in any Manner affect the first and fourth Clauses in the Ninth Section of the first Article; and that no State, without its Consent, shall be deprived of its equal Suffrage in the Senate.

Article VI (Article 6 - Prior Debts, National Supremacy, Oaths of Office)

1. All Debts contracted and Engagements entered into, before the Adoption of this Constitution, shall be as valid against the United States under this Constitution, as under the Confederation.
2. This Constitution, and the Laws of the United States which shall be made in Pursuance thereof; and all Treaties made, or which shall be made, under the Authority of the United States, shall be the supreme Law of the Land; and the Judges in every State shall be bound thereby, any Thing in the Constitution or Laws of any State to the Contrary notwithstanding.
3. The Senators and Representatives before mentioned, and the Members of the several State Legislatures, and all executive and judicial Officers, both of the United States and of the several States, shall be bound by Oath or Affirmation, to support this Constitution; but no religious

Test shall ever be required as a Qualification to any Office or public Trust under the United States.

Article VII (Article 7 - Ratification)

The Ratification of the Conventions of nine States, shall be sufficient for the Establishment of this Constitution between the States so ratifying the Same.

The Word "the", being interlined between the seventh and eight Lines of the first Page, The Word "Thirty" being partly written on an Erazure in the fifteenth Line of the first Page. The Words "is tried" being interlined between the thirty second and thirty third Lines of the first Page and the Word "the" being interlined between the forty third and forty fourth Lines of the second Page.

done in Convention by the Unanimous Consent of the States present the Seventeenth Day of September in the Year of our Lord on thousand seven hundred and Eighty seven and the Independence of the United States of America the Twelfth In witness whereof We have hereunto subscribed our Names,

Attest William Jackson

Secretary

G°: Washington - Presid^t. and deputy from Virginia

Delaware

Geo: Read

Gunning Bedford jun

John Dickson

Richard Bassett

Jaco: Broom

Maryland

James McHenry

Dan of S.^tTho.^s Jenifer

Danl Carroll.

Virginia

John Blair

James Madison Jr.

North Carolina

Wm Blount

Richd Dobbs Spaight

Hu Williamson

South Carolina

J. Rutledge

Charles Cotesworth Pinckney

Charles Pinckney

Pierce Butler

Georgia

William Few

Abr Baldwin

New Hampshire

John Langdon

Nicholas Gilman

Massachusetts

Nathaniel Gorham

Rufus King

Connecticut

W^m. Saml. Johnson

Roger Sherman

New York

Alexander Hamilton

New Jersey

Wil. Livingston

David Brearley.

W^m. Paterson.

Jona: Dayton

Pennsylvania

B Franklin

Thomas Mifflin

Robt Morris

Geo. Clymer

Thos. FitzSimons

Jared Ingersoll

James Wilson

Gouv Morris

Congress of the United States

Begun and held at the City of New-York on Wednesday the fourth of March, one thousand seven hundred and eighty nine.

THE Conventions of a number of the States, having at the time of their adopting the Constitution, expressed a desire, in order to prevent misconstruction or abuse of its powers, that further declaratory and restrictive clauses should be added: And as extending the ground of public confidence in the Government, will best ensure the beneficent ends of its institution.

RESOLVED by the Senate and House of Representatives of the United States of America, in Congress assembled, two thirds of both Houses concurring, that the following Articles be proposed to the Legislatures of the several States, as amendments to the Constitution of the United States, all, or any of which Articles, when ratified by three fourths of the said Legislatures, to be valid to all intents and purposes, as part of the said Constitution; viz.

The Constitution

ARTICLES in addition to, and Amendment of the Constitution of the United States of America, proposed by Congress, and ratified by the Legislatures of the several States, pursuant to the fifth Article of the original Constitution.

Article the first. ..... After the first enumeration required by the first Article of the Constitution, there shall be one Representative for every thirty thousand, until the number shall amount to one hundred, after which, the proportion shall be so regulated by Congress, that there shall be not less than one hundred Representatives, nor less than one Representative for every forty thousand persons, until the number of Representatives shall amount to two hundred, after which the proportion shall be so regulated by Congress, that there shall not be less than two hundred Representatives, nor more than one Representative for every fifty thousand persons.

Article the second. .... No law, varying the compensation for the services of the Senators and Representatives, shall take effect, until an election of Representatives shall have intervened

The Bill of Rights

Article I

Congress shall make no law respecting an establishment of religion, or prohibiting the free exercise thereof; or abridging the freedom of speech, or of the press; or the right of the people peaceably to assemble, and to petition the Government for a redress of grievances.

Article II

A well regulated Militia, being necessary to the security of a free State, the right of the people to keep and bear Arms, shall not be infringed.

Article III

No Soldier shall, in time of peace be quartered in any house, without the consent of the Owner, nor in time of war, but in a manner to be prescribed by law.

The Bill of Rights

Article IV

The right of the people to be secure in their persons, houses, papers, and effects, against unreasonable searches and seizures, shall not be violated, and no Warrants shall issue, but upon probable cause, supported by Oath or affirmation, and particularly describing the place to be searched, and the persons or things to be seized.

Article V

No person shall be held to answer for a capital, or otherwise infamous crime, unless on a presentment or indictment of a Grand Jury, except in cases arising in the land or naval forces, or in the Militia, when in actual service in time of War or public danger; nor shall any person be subject for the same offence to be twice put in jeopardy of life or limb; nor shall be compelled in any criminal case to be a witness against himself, nor be deprived of life, liberty, or property, without due process of law; nor shall private property be taken for public use, without just compensation.

Article VI

In all criminal prosecutions, the accused shall enjoy the right to a speedy and public trial, by an impartial jury of the State and district wherein the crime shall have been committed, which district shall have been previously ascertained by law, and to be informed of the nature and cause of the accusation; to be confronted with the witnesses against him; to have compulsory process for obtaining witnesses in his favor, and to have the Assistance of Counsel for his defence.

Article VII

In Suits at common law, where the value in controversy shall exceed twenty dollars, the right of trial by jury shall be preserved, and no fact tried by a jury, shall be otherwise re-examined in any Court of the United States, than according to the rules of the common law.

Article VIII

Excessive bail shall not be required, nor excessive fines imposed, nor cruel and unusual punishments inflicted.

Article IX

The enumeration in the Constitution, of certain rights, shall not be construed to deny or disparage others retained by the people.

Article X

The powers not delegated to the United States by the Constitution, nor prohibited by it to the States, are reserved to the States respectively, or to the people.

Attest,
John Beckley, Clerk of the House of Representatives.
Sam. A. Otis Secretary of the Senate.

Frederick Augustus Muhlenberg Speaker of the House of Representatives.
John Adams, Vice-President of the

The Bill of Rights

United States, and
President of the
Senate.

Amendments 11 thru 27

Article XI

The Judicial power of the United States shall not be construed to extend to any suit in law or equity, commenced or prosecuted against one of the United States by Citizens of another State, or by Citizens or Subjects of any Foreign State.

Article XII

The Electors shall meet in their respective states, and vote by ballot for President and Vice-President, one of whom, at least, shall not be an inhabitant of the same state with themselves; they shall name in their ballots the person voted for as President, and in distinct ballots the person voted for as Vice-President, and they shall make distinct lists of all persons voted for as President, and of all persons voted for as Vice-President, and of the number of votes for each, which lists they shall sign and certify, and transmit sealed to the seat of the government of the United States, directed to the President of the Senate; — The President of the Senate shall, in the presence of the Senate and House of Representatives, open all the certificates and the votes shall then be counted; — The person having the greatest number of votes for President, shall be the President, if such number be a majority of the whole number of Electors appointed; and if no person have such majority, then from the persons having the highest numbers not exceeding three on the list of those voted for as President, the House of Representatives shall choose immediately, by ballot, the President. But in choosing the President, the votes shall be taken by states, the representation from each state having one vote; a quorum for this purpose shall consist of a member or members from two-thirds of the states, and a majority of all the states shall be necessary to a choice. And if the House of Representatives shall not choose a President whenever the right of choice shall devolve upon them, before the fourth day of March next following, then the Vice-President shall act as President, as in the case of the death or other constitutional disability of the President. — The person having the greatest number of votes as Vice-President, shall be the Vice-President, if such number be a majority of the whole number of Electors appointed, and if no person have a majority, then from the two highest numbers on the list, the Senate shall choose the Vice-President; a quorum for the purpose shall consist of two-thirds of the whole number of Senators, and a majority of the whole number shall be necessary to a choice. But no person constitutionally ineligible to the office of President shall be eligible to that of Vice-President of the United States.

Article XIII

Neither slavery nor involuntary servitude, except as a punishment for crime whereof the party shall have been duly convicted, shall exist within the United States, or any place subject to their jurisdiction.

Congress shall have power to enforce this article by appropriate legislation.

Article XIV

1. All persons born or naturalized in the United States, and subject to the jurisdiction thereof, are citizens of the United States and of the State wherein they reside. No State shall make or enforce any law which shall abridge the privileges or immunities of citizens of the United States; nor shall any State deprive any person of life, liberty, or property, without due process of law; nor deny to any person within its jurisdiction the equal protection of the laws.
2. Representatives shall be apportioned among the several States according to their respective numbers, counting the whole number of persons in each State, excluding Indians not taxed. But when the right to vote at any election for the choice of electors for President and Vice President of the United States, Representatives in Congress, the Executive and Judicial officers of a State, or the members of the Legislature thereof, is denied to any of the male inhabitants of such State, being twenty-one years of age, and citizens of the United States, or in any way abridged, except for participation in rebellion, or other crime, the basis of representation therein shall be reduced in the

proportion which the number of such male citizens shall bear to the whole number of male citizens twenty-one years of age in such State.
3. No person shall be a Senator or Representative in Congress, or elector of President and Vice President, or hold any office, civil or military, under the United States, or under any State, who, having previously taken an oath, as a member of Congress, or as an officer of the United States, or as a member of any State legislature, or as an executive or judicial officer of any State, to support the Constitution of the United States, shall have engaged in insurrection or rebellion against the same, or given aid or comfort to the enemies thereof. But Congress may by a vote of two-thirds of each House, remove such disability.
4. The validity of the public debt of the United States, authorized by law, including debts incurred for payment of pensions and bounties for services in suppressing insurrection or rebellion, shall not be questioned. But neither the United States nor any State shall assume or pay any debt or obligation incurred in aid of insurrection or rebellion against the United States, or any claim for the loss or emancipation of any slave; but all such debts, obligations and claims shall be held illegal and void.
5. The Congress shall have power to enforce, by appropriate legislation, the provisions of this article.

Article XV

The right of citizens of the United States to vote shall not be denied or abridged by the United States or by any State on account of race, color, or previous condition of servitude.

The Congress shall have power to enforce this article by appropriate legislation.

Article XVI

The Congress shall have power to lay and collect taxes on incomes, from whatever source derived, without apportionment among the several States, and without regard to any census or enumeration.

Article XVII

1. The Senate of the United States shall be composed of two Senators from each State, elected by the people thereof, for six years; and each Senator shall have one vote. The electors in each State shall have the qualifications requisite for electors of the most numerous branch of the State legislatures.
2. When vacancies happen in the representation of any State in the Senate, the executive authority of such State shall issue writs of election to fill such vacancies: Provided, That the legislature of any State may empower the executive thereof to make temporary appointments until the people fill the vacancies by election as the legislature may direct.
3. This amendment shall not be so construed as to affect the election or term of any Senator chosen before it becomes valid as part of the Constitution.

Article XVIII

1. After one year from the ratification of this article the manufacture, sale, or transportation of intoxicating liquors within, the importation thereof into, or the exportation thereof from the United States and all territory subject to

the jurisdiction thereof for beverage purposes is hereby prohibited.
2. The Congress and the several States shall have concurrent power to enforce this article by appropriate legislation.
3. This article shall be inoperative unless it shall have been ratified as an amendment to the Constitution by the legislatures of the several States, as provided in the Constitution, within seven years from the date of the submission hereof to the States by the Congress.

Article XIX

The right of citizens of the United States to vote shall not be denied or abridged by the United States or by any State on account of sex.

Congress shall have power to enforce this article by appropriate legislation.

Article XX

1. The terms of the President and Vice President shall end at noon on the 20th day of January, and the terms of Senators and Representatives at noon on the 3d day of January, of the years in which such terms would have ended if this article had not been ratified; and the terms of their successors shall then begin.
2. The Congress shall assemble at least once in every year, and such meeting shall begin at noon on the 3d day of January, unless they shall by law appoint a different day.
3. If, at the time fixed for the beginning of the term of the President, the President elect shall have died, the Vice President elect shall become President. If a President shall not have been chosen before the time fixed for the

beginning of his term, or if the President elect shall have failed to qualify, then the Vice President elect shall act as President until a President shall have qualified; and the Congress may by law provide for the case wherein neither a President elect nor a Vice President elect shall have qualified, declaring who shall then act as President, or the manner in which one who is to act shall be selected, and such person shall act accordingly until a President or Vice President shall have qualified.

4. The Congress may by law provide for the case of the death of any of the persons from whom the House of Representatives may choose a President whenever the right of choice shall have devolved upon them, and for the case of the death of any of the persons from whom the Senate may choose a Vice President whenever the right of choice shall have devolved upon them.
5. Sections 1 and 2 shall take effect on the 15th day of October following the ratification of this article.
6. This article shall be inoperative unless it shall have been ratified as an amendment to the Constitution by the legislatures of three-fourths of the several States within seven years from the date of its submission.

Article XXI

1. The eighteenth article of amendment to the Constitution of the United States is hereby repealed. affects 16
2. The transportation or importation into any State, Territory, or possession of the United States for delivery or use therein of intoxicating liquors, in violation of the laws thereof, is hereby prohibited.

3. This article shall be inoperative unless it shall have been ratified as an amendment to the Constitution by conventions in the several States, as provided in the Constitution, within seven years from the date of the submission hereof to the States by the Congress.

Amendment XXII

1. No person shall be elected to the office of the President more than twice, and no person who has held the office of President, or acted as President, for more than two years of a term to which some other person was elected President shall be elected to the office of the President more than once. But this article shall not apply to any person holding the office of President when this article was proposed by the Congress, and shall not prevent any person who may be holding the office of President, or acting as President, during the term within which this article becomes operative from holding the office of President or acting as President during the remainder of such term.
2. This article shall be inoperative unless it shall have been ratified as an amendment to the Constitution by the legislatures of three-fourths of the several states within seven years from the date of its submission to the states by the Congress.

Amendment XXIII

1. The District constituting the seat of government of the United States shall appoint in such manner as the Congress may direct: A number of electors of President and Vice President equal to the whole number of Senators

and Representatives in Congress to which the District would be entitled if it were a state, but in no event more than the least populous state; they shall be in addition to those appointed by the states, but they shall be considered, for the purposes of the election of President and Vice President, to be electors appointed by a state; and they shall meet in the District and perform such duties as provided by the twelfth article of amendment.

2. The Congress shall have power to enforce this article by appropriate legislation.

Amendment XXIV

1. The right of citizens of the United States to vote in any primary or other election for President or Vice President, for electors for President or Vice President, or for Senator or Representative in Congress, shall not be denied or abridged by the United States or any state by reason of failure to pay any poll tax or other tax.
2. The Congress shall have power to enforce this article by appropriate legislation.

Amendment XXV

1. In case of the removal of the President from office or of his death or resignation, the Vice President shall become President.
2. Whenever there is a vacancy in the office of the Vice President, the President shall nominate a Vice President who shall take office upon confirmation by a majority vote of both Houses of Congress.
3. Whenever the President transmits to the President pro tempore of the Senate and the Speaker of the House of

Representatives his written declaration that he is unable to discharge the powers and duties of his office, and until he transmits to them a written declaration to the contrary, such powers and duties shall be discharged by the Vice President as Acting President.

4. Whenever the Vice President and a majority of either the principal officers of the executive departments or of such other body as Congress may by law provide, transmit to the President pro tempore of the Senate and the Speaker of the House of Representatives their written declaration that the President is unable to discharge the powers and duties of his office, the Vice President shall immediately assume the powers and duties of the office as Acting President.

Thereafter, when the President transmits to the President pro tempore of the Senate and the Speaker of the House of Representatives his written declaration that no inability exists, he shall resume the powers and duties of his office unless the Vice President and a majority of either the principal officers of the executive department or of such other body as Congress may by law provide, transmit within four days to the President pro tempore of the Senate and the Speaker of the House of Representatives their written declaration that the President is unable to discharge the powers and duties of his office. Thereupon Congress shall decide the issue, assembling within forty-eight hours for that purpose if not in session. If the Congress, within twenty-one days after receipt of the latter written declaration, or, if Congress is not in session, within twenty-one days after Congress is required to assemble, determines by two-thirds vote of both Houses that the President is unable to discharge the powers and duties of his office, the Vice President shall continue to discharge the same as Acting President; otherwise, the President shall resume the powers and duties of his office.

Amendment XXVI

1. The right of citizens of the United States, who are 18 years of age or older, to vote, shall not be denied or abridged by the United States or any state on account of age.
2. The Congress shall have the power to enforce this article by appropriate legislation.

Amendment XXVII

No law varying the compensation for the services of the Senators and Representatives shall take effect until an election of Representatives shall have intervened.

From the Top

Let's begin at the beginning. We the People. That's what it says. That should be sufficiently simple and straightforward, even for members of the Supreme Court. Sadly, that isn't the case.

Most reading this think that the United States is a democracy. Not true. Well, not exactly true. To put matters in perspective, this nation is an experiment. Prior to our independence, republics had a poor track record. The Caesars took over and trashed the Roman Republic.

This is probably the place to provide a couple of definitions. We all have heard many times some pompous-axx lecture all about that this is a republic, not a democracy. While, in his hubris, he thinks that he is enlightening us poor benighted souls with his unlimited wisdom; he is actually displaying his ignorance of the definitions of both terms.

There are two types of government: monarchy and republic. The former is hereditary, while the later is nonhereditary. It's as simple as that, but apparently over the heads for those spouting that little piece of *faux* wisdom.

Democracy is an option for decision-making for either a monarchy or a republic. Theoretically, it is a way of allowing those affected by governmental decisions to participate in the making of those decisions. Remember, it is only theoretical.

While children, even the yet to be born, are often affected by the many decisions we make, we have reasons for not letting grammar school students out of class to help elect the president. The unborn present a fairly difficult problem in how to determine their preferences.

Those in other countries are often affected by the decisions of our leaders but few of you want to extend the franchise to all of those 'aliens.'

What some credit as the first democracy was in Greece. Their democracy was hardly extended generously. No women or other slaves were permitted to participate. Both women and slaves were considered to be property. Everyone knew that property couldn't vote.

However, following the case known as Citizens United *vs*. Federal Election Commission, when the Supreme Court created the 'right' of corporations to exercise 'their' freedom of speech under the First Amendment, that verity is now in doubt.

You say that can't be? As Jack Paar (predecessor to Johnny Carson on the Tonight Show) was famous for saying, "I kid you not."

In 2010, in the case of Citizens United *vs*. Federal Election Commission, those Constitutional scholars created a right of corporations to exercise 'their' freedom of speech under the First Amendment.

This also extends, separate from the Fifth Amendment right against self-incrimination, equal protections under the law to corporations. Therefore, in the case of Burwell *vs*. Hobby Lobby Stores, Inc., corporations had religious rights under the falsely-named 'Religious Freedom Restoration Act.' This extended the corporations an exemption from the Patient Protection and Affordable Care Act aka Obamacare.

The result was that the creativity of the Court's majority permitted the owners of corporations to deny health coverage for employees that they considered at odds with their convenient religion.

My personal belief is that corporations should lose their religious right to discriminate if the corporation misses weekly services at their local church, temple or mosque three or more weeks in a row.

Understand that the decision to hold corporations to have the same rights as actual humans is not without problems. This is because the Court actually created a class of elite 'people,' people who cannot be imprisoned or executed. They could be but won't be.

Back to the ancients in Greece. All decisions were shared by whoever showed up at the proper time. That was not very efficient. If 537 eligible citizens showed up for a trial, you had a jury of 537.

Their version of democracy did have one feature that should be emulated here. Once a year, with a quorum of at least 6,000, they could vote to exile any citizen. If a majority agreed, they would be expelled for 10 years.

This was not used as punishment for a crime. It was used primarily against the elite if they were seen as a danger to the democracy, by trying to gather to themselves too much power and influence. I would wager most readers could name a few prospective candidates for that treatment.

Fear of Corporations

Corporations being everywhere since long before our times, they seem just a fact of life. They don't just fade into the background; they are the background. Do they need to be? Are they necessary? Are they benign?

You may have heard of the Boston Tea Party. Have you ever asked whose tea was thrown into the harbor? It belonged to a corporation, the East India Company.

It was chartered by Queen Elizabeth I in 1600. Back then, severe restrictions were placed on all corporations. They were formed for a limited period of time – usually 15 to 30 years, for a specific purpose. The East India Company eventually became an agency of the British Indian government in 1834.

They were formed for a specific purpose – to counter the Dutch East Indies Company's monopoly of the spice trade in Indonesia. They had their own military arm and used it frequently – once they went to war against their French counterpart, in 1752 and against their Dutch rivals in 1759. We won't count those times their arms were turned on the local citizenry.

Some of the other restrictions were prohibitions against political, or even charitable, contributions. They could not own stock in other corporations or have interlocking boards. I'm unaware of any corporation that today meets those requirements. Most states at the founding made political contributions a crime. I would welcome them back.

The creation of corporations was to provide benefits to the society that required large amounts of money. To be of such benefit necessitated that they be large. Large was feared back in the day. Therefore, the multitude of restrictions. Often, even profits were limited on most. That one didn't survive very long.

As evidenced by the Boston Tea Party, corporations won few popularity contests. All of the fears were realized. As wealth piled up, it was used to purchase the government. At the time of the Revolution, almost every member of parliament owned stock in the East India Company.

It may be that some of this is new to some readers, but it caused longstanding grievances among the Founding Fathers. Thomas Jefferson said he hoped to "crush in its birth the aristocracy of our monied corporations, which dare already to challenge our government to a trial of strength and bid defiance to the laws of our country."

Then there was James Madison, the primary creator of the Constitution, who wrote that "incorporated companies with proper limitations and guards may, in particular cases, be useful; but they are at best a necessary evil only."

And Thomas Paine, "But charters and corporations have a more extensive evil effect than what relates merely to elections. They are sources of endless contentions in places where they exist, and they lessen the common rights of national society."

All of that helps explain the reasons for celebrating "We the People."

Welfare

Yes, Virginia, much to the chagrin of those people calling themselves conservatives, according to the Constitution a prominent reason for establishing the United States was to provide for the general welfare. It's right there in the very first sentence.

The primary reason for forming a government is for it to do for you that which you cannot do for yourself or because it can handle some concerns better or more effectively than we can individually. If at my tender age I could not produce the wherewithal to feed myself, Social Security would come in handy. Since I have paid into it for a lifetime, that, strictly speaking, isn't welfare. Though, if Social Security didn't exist, not allowing droves of geezers' bodies to litter the streets would require some degree of welfare.

At my age, were it not for doctors' appointments, I wouldn't have a social life. I have multiple maladies, without the expertise and resources to heal myself. When I recently became paralyzed in both legs, I was in a rehabilitation center for 91 days. Even with Medicare I received a bill for almost $13,000. Not every senior is able to absorb such a financial hit. I, myself, was on the cusp.

Parts of the Government

Following the short preamble, the Constitution gets down to business. Starting with the legislature, it lays out the obligations and boundaries of the three branches of government.

For some reason, most likely an overly simplistic reading the document, the three branches are almost universally described as being coequal. They are not.

The authors of the Constitution were members of the elite. They knew the power of money. So, they gave what they considered the power of the purse to the only part of the government that was elected directly by the people, the House of Representatives. That puts the House in the driver's seat.

While the Senate has to be content with giving or withholding 'Advice and Consent,' The executive does get to execute whatever the Congress tells it to do. Meanwhile, the Supreme Court waits for the others to disagree for it to make the wrong decision about half the time. It could probably be replaced with one person flipping a coin (the black robe optional).

Those old guys, the Founding Fathers, were pretty smart. They put the various components in their order of importance. First, we find the people. Next, there is the legislature. First inside of that is the House – then the Senate. They do remember the positions of lesser importance – the president and those wearing a somber costume.

The House can impeach and the Senate can convict to rid us of any officer of the federal government. Their jurisdiction includes the president and members of the Supreme Court. Neither the president nor the Supreme Court can boot any member of Congress. Does that sound 'coequal?'

There are several checks and balances but nothing 'coequal.'

Legislation

In the following sentence, Section 1, it states that:

All legislative Powers herein granted shall be vested in a Congress of the United States, which shall consist of a Senate and House of Representatives.

The legislative branch makes the laws. It also decides how your money is to be spent. That is the case whether you like how they spend your money or not. And, that is the case whether the president likes it or not.

The president operates the executive branch. Why have an executive branch? Because someone has to implement the decisions of the legislative branch. So, among the president's responsibilities is the duty to make happen the desires of the legislative branch.

If the legislature says, spend this much here and don't spend any over there, the president's job description requires him or her to spend this much here and nothing over there.

There is some discretion permitted but it is limited. Some monies allocated to the Department of Defense, for instance, may be shifted from one project to another when justified. That discretion does not extend to shifting those monies to a different department. Dollars designated for military use cannot be reallocated to civilian projects without the agreement of the legislature. Think "the wall."

Democracy?

I may as well address this matter early on.

Section 3 covers the Senate. As you learned in grammar school, the Senate is composed of two delegates from each state. That hardly seems in tune with democracy. It isn't, by a long shot.

California has two senators. Wyoming has two senators. California has 68.25 times as many people as Wyoming. That two per state carries over to the Electoral College. We all know how wonderfully that has worked out. Giving the presidency to the loser is not how an actual democracy is supposed to work.

It's a shame that schools have eliminated the requirement of sitting in a civics class for a year. In discussions of the College following the debacle of the 2016 election, I was surprised to hear the compulsory pontificating talking heads explain that it was created because of slavery.

I guess I'll have to give them partial credit. Ratification of the Constitution required nine votes. The small states were apprehensive. They did not relish the thought of having little, if any, say in the governance of this new nation. Therefore, the Senate was created as a compromise to get the agreement of the small states.

Why partial credit? The southern states, being agricultural, that is rural, though sizeable in terms of acreage, were in much the same position of the tiny states. They were able to wrangle two concessions.

If slaves were counted, the population was increased. In another compromise each slave counted as three-fifths of a human being. So, though it involved a concession to the slave-holding states, the purpose was to get the votes of those states for ratification.

Lest we forget, the required super-majorities of sixty percent and two-thirds are also meant to frustrate democratic majorities. Each house of

Congress creates various rules that also restrict an actual democracy.

No, Virginia, this representative democracy we have is that in little more than name only. It has been grossly distorted, corrupted. The elite didn't fully trust the rabble to govern ourselves. Do I exaggerate? How many politicians are owned by someone other than you?

Democracy is much more aspiration than fact.

Emoluments

Emoluments must have been considered important to the Founders. After all, they included it in the Constitution twice. You will find it as regards foreign sources in Article 1, Section 9. Then, it appears again as regards domestic sources in Article 2, Section 1.

The definition is straightforward. A salary, fee, or profit from employment or office. Obviously, the president should be paid a salary. This salary shall be paid by the Treasury.

The Constitution addresses emoluments from other sources. "No Title of Nobility shall be granted by the United States: And no Person holding any Office of Profit or Trust under them, shall, without the Consent of the Congress, accept of any present, Emolument, Office, or Title, of any kind whatever, from any King, Prince, or foreign

State." The other mention is to bar any emolument being received from any of the states.

The reason for this restriction is obvious. Anyone giving anything of value to the president just might be able to exert undue influence on him/her. Though I have mentioned only the president so far, the quotation shows that it applies to any person holding any office of profit or trust under the United States or any of the individual states.

Our present president refuses to play by the rules. He intends to profit from the office. Though he and his family have already found multiple ways of scamming, grifting, swindling and otherwise profiting from their positions, the elephant in the room is Trump's hotel just down the street from our White House.

Trump leases that property from the federal government, which makes him his own landlord. Although I would not spend too much time in such an obvious target for terrorists, many book rooms there with the expectation of making Trump happy by putting money in his pockets. My guess is that the odds are in their favor. However, all such emoluments are barred. It does not depend on whether the bribes are successful of influencing the president.

Several lawsuits have been and will be filed in this matter. The State of Maryland and the District of Columbia have brought suit because the hotel has an unfair advantage over its competition.

Some judges wish to require petitioners to show that they have standing. That means that they are negatively affected.

One would think that, since the Constitution begins with "We the People," every citizen is negatively affected by a violation of it. Members of Congress certainly have standing and are suing, as do others.

Pardon Me

There have been some claims made that the president can pardon himself/herself. You might think it was made in jest. Not so.

When people see a personal catastrophe looming, they grasp at any straw, real or imagined. Pardoning someone for the crime for which they were convicted should be used to correct an obvious wrong; if a person was wrongfully convicted or the punishment was too harsh for the offense or for humanitarian reasons. But, no one is supposed to be above the law.

The pardon was not intended as an escape from justice. To allow a president to pardon himself/herself would be comparable to permitting ordinary convicted felons to excuse themselves from whatever sentence was meted out to them.

In the same vein, no government official is allowed to use his/her office to commit a crime. Offering, much less giving, a pardon to someone in order to obstruct justice is likewise prohibited, for the self-same reason.

On this subject, I have a real problem with Gerald Ford's Pardon of Nixon. There was nothing to pardon Nixon for, as he had yet to be convicted of a crime. Also, Ford pardoned Nixon for any possible future crimes. That was a bridge too far, or two bridges.

Religion

Religion is and has been a problem for millennia. It has been a problem both here and around the world. The wrong religion could result in one being killed, run out of the country and dispossessed or even unpleasant impositions.

Baptists are fairly well established now but, in colonial days, one could be imprisoned in North Carolina just for preaching the Baptist version of Christianity.

Meanwhile, other states paid the salaries of preachers of the Anglican or Presbyterian persuasion. The need for a change in the rules of the games were obvious.

It was seen that both of the above situations were unfair. The government should be neutral. The preferred stance for the government was to get out of the game. There should be no involvement.

Here was a situation where a wall actually made sense.

Well, you may have noticed that you can't please everyone. Even back then they were plagued by true-believers. True-believers tend to err on the side of passion, zealotry, fanaticism or bias.

Many of this frame of mind have sought special status from the conception of the nation to the present day. If they fail to get their way, they are prepared to behave in the famous 'cry-baby' mode and claim the role of victim.

Victim? Surely they jest. Living in the Bible Belt, it seems there are few corners not the home of a church. A politician dares not omit mention of his faith in any oration. It must be repeated at least every 97 seconds.

It's difficult to credit the claim that Christianity is under attack when 70 to 80 percent of the population identifies as Christian. Just a thought; ask anyone what year this is. It appears that Christianity is the winner, not the victim.

Those 'cry-babies' wish the government to do their work for them, by imposing their positions on abortion, sexuality and such on those who fail to agree. It is difficult to see them as Christians or patriotic Americans, as they deny the tenets of the teachings of both the New Testament and the Constitution.

They also demand a small government. Is it one small enough for them to ignore with impunity or one small enough to sneak into your bedroom or both? Our population and global responsibilities are large and complex. A small government is a fool's pipe dream.

The separation of church and state is intended to protect the church from the state fighting either for or against it while also protecting the state from interference by the church.

The intent of the Founders was to eliminate any possibility of this being or becoming a theocracy (think Iran) or establishing a state-sponsored religion. Those wishing for the United States to be a "Christian" nation should consider the possibilities. Just which version would the government choose; the Catholic church or the Snake-handling Baptists?

There is one obvious breach of the separation which is rarely mentioned. Religious property is exempt from taxation. These properties benefit from various government services. They enjoy the infrastructure and such services as the police and fire departments.

Those government services cost money. Even if some property is not required to pay for them, they still must be paid for. That means a greater tax burden on all other property. It also means that a Baptist must subsidize Catholic churches, Jewish synagogues, Muslim mosques and the facilities of the Sikhs and even of the Methodists.

This breach belies the claim that these religion bodies are independent. Kids going off to college certainly feel independent, but are they? If daddy is paying for room, board and tuition, that student cannot honestly claim to be independent.

If the government is subsidizing these religious bodies, there is no separation or independence. The government would be totally justified in interfering in any manner, but for the Constitution. It must be one way or the other.

The 2nd Amendment

I doubt that any other part of the Constitution has been or could be subject to more distortion and deliberate misunderstanding than the 2nd Amendment. The knuckle-draggers ignore history and the actual wording of it and torture language and logic to get their way. They also buy Congressmen.

The National Rifle Association makes lots of noise and claims to own this Amendment. They also claim to have 5 million members. No one believes that number. Even so, that would be only 6-7 percent of gunowners in this country.

Their claim to represent gun owners is also specious. While the organization vehemently resists registration by gun owners, 73 percent of their membership favors registration. Their 'representation' is pretty much on a par with Congress representing its citizenry.

Let's do something different. Let's look at the facts. The Founders feared a standing army, with good reason. Standing armies are the foundation of *coups d'état*.

Though they won independence from the British, a large portion of the public still considered themselves loyalists. The Articles of Confederation failed to provide a strong government. That was the reason for establishing a brand-new government under a brand-new Constitution. A weak government with a divided populace could invite an attempt to overthrow it.

How could you have a military capability without a standing army? A Militia. Arm all of those farmers, small business owners, clerks, *et al*. Let them bear arms only when an armed force was needed. Organized by state, a unified force with a national goal was less likely to endanger the new federal government.

The ones interpreting the Amendment as a gift from the Founders for fighting against the government defy logic and history, not the government.

The 2nd Amendment

Remember that the Founding Fathers pledged their lives, their fortunes and their sacred honor to bring this government into being. It is dumbfounding to consider a postulation that these selfsame Founders would put into the Constitution a mechanism to enable a bunch of dimwits to destroy what they were willing to give everything to realize.

It's hard to accept that some of these people think its possible for them to go up against the array of weaponry that the government has. An AK-47 isn't exactly an equalizer for a drone, a tank, *et al.*

Gun owners should be grateful that the government permits them to have guns for sport, hunting and self-protection. The Constitution doesn't require them to.

States' Rights?

The following quotation is the 10th Amendment. Its poor wording has provided an opportunity for gross misinterpretation. It has been used primarily to support slavery, segregation, denial of abortion and other such misbegotten nonsense.

The powers not delegated to the United States by the Constitution, nor prohibited by it to the States, are reserved to the States respectively, or to the people.

People have rights. Governments don't. They have responsibilities. At least that's the way it is supposed to be.

Governments would not exist but for people. Governments are created of, by and for people. Governments do have powers. They have the powers that people cede to them. That is the way it is supposed to be.

Many, perhaps all, governments have taken rights. A major purpose of the Constitution was to ensure that the people retain those rights.

Shutting Down

Back in 1917, in the midst of World War I, Congress instituted a debt limit. Rather than have the honesty to give the bill its own name, they put it into the Second Liberty Bond Act of 1917.

It provided that Congress had to specifically permit the Treasury to borrow more money to pay the bills.

You may recall, our focus here is on the Constitution. Congressional bills have no validity unless they conform to the Constitution. Does the Second Liberty Bond Act conform?

No.

When it is used as the excuse, *ipso facto*, shutting down the government violates the Constitution.

Where does the Constitution say that? Since it is not where one would expect it to be, all of those experts inside the Beltway miss it, either due to not having read it . . . or, intentionally.

There it is, plain as the nose on your face: The Fourteenth Amendment, Section 2.

The validity of the public debt of the United States, authorized by law, including debts incurred for payment of pensions and bounties for services in suppressing insurrection or rebellion, shall not be questioned.

The public debt, all of it, no exceptions, shall not be questioned. That just means that legal debts must be honored, must be paid.

So, what is legal debt? Every last cent of our debt is legal. Why? Because every last cent of our debt results from a bill passed by both the House and Senate and signed by the president. That makes them legal.

If Congress and the president authorized a debt, the Treasurer must not question it. If the Treasury is paying all of the government's bills, the spurious claim that Congress has not authorized the Treasurer to borrow enough money to pay the bills is totally without merit. By the acts of passing bills costing money the Congress and the president have incurred debts that must be honored.

That, of course, includes payment of salaries to all employees of the government and the contractees.

If the debt limit is unconstitutional, there is no excuse for shutting down the government. How can the people sworn to govern on our behalf govern if the government is shut down?

From the Publisher

Essential books is a new publisher. The initial goal is to bring out four books annually. This is our second.

If you enjoyed or profited from this work, we would appreciate a review – five stars, of course. Actually, we would appreciate a five-star review even if you didn't enjoy it.

Our website is still basic at this point but you can watch it develop by stopping by occasionally. Questions, suggestions, criticisms or other comments are welcome.

We are trying to get the URL that matches our company name, so pay no attention to the actual URL. You can find us at essentialbooks.online

The Author

Crawford claims to be so old that the ringing in his ears was caused by the Big Bang. He has far too much education for his own good and too much experience to defer to the powers that be. Despite being a political oddity there, he is from Tennessee, from the place where the sun shines bright and the moonshine's delicious.

His experience includes holding public elective office, as well as being executive director for a nonprofit, a foreign correspondent, writing for an academic journal, working for military intelligence and being homeless, back in the 1950s, before it became so popular.

Academically, he was a tenured student, specializing in almost everything: math, physics, anthropology, history, political science, law, sociology and psychology. His graduate studies were in international relations and international economics. He still hasn't decided what he wants to be when he grows up, if ever.

Crawford holds eight patents and lost a fortune trying to monetize one of them. He finally learned the truth of the old saying, that a patent only gives you the right to sue, but not necessarily successfully.

www.ingramcontent.com/pod-product-compliance
Lightning Source LLC
Chambersburg PA
CBHW071312060426
42444CB00034B/1977